LET'S L  S

LET'S LOOK AT SOMALIA

BY A. M. REYNOLDS

CAPSTONE PRESS
a capstone imprint

Pebble Plus is published by Capstone Press,
1710 Roe Crest Drive, North Mankato, Minnesota 56003
www.mycapstone.com

Library of Congress Cataloging-in-Publication Data
Names: Reynolds, A. M., 1958– author.
Title: Let's look at Somalia / by A.M. Reynolds.
Description: North Mankato, Minn. : Capstone Press, 2019. | Series: Pebble plus. Let's look at countries |Identifiers: LCCN 2018029940 (print) | LCCN 2018031754 (ebook) | ISBN 9781977103949 (eBook PDF) | ISBN 9781977103857 (hardcover) | ISBN 9781977105646 (pbk.)
Subjects: LCSH: Somalia—Juvenile literature.
Classification: LCC DT401.5 (ebook) | LCC DT401.5 .R49 2019 (print) | DDC 967.73—dc23
LC record available at https://lccn.loc.gov/2018029940

Editorial Credits
Erika L. Shores, editor; Juliette Peters, designer; Jo Miller, media researcher;
Laura Manthe, production specialist

Photo Credits
Alamy: Angela Fitch, 8; Dreamstime: Patrick Wangari, Cover Bottom; iStockphoto: muendo, 9; Newscom: Reuters/Feisal Omar, 1, 15, Cover Top, Reuters/Omar Faruk, 13, Reuters/STR, 12, robertharding/Liba Taylor, 16, 17, Universal Images Group/De Agostini/A. Tessore, 3; Shutterstock: Afonso Martins, Cover Middle, Cover Back, Free Wind 2014, 19, 22-23, 24, Globe Turner, 22 (Inset), HelloRF Zcool, 6, Homo Cosmicos, 20, imeduard, 21, nate, 4; Wikimedia: AMISOM Photo / Ilyas Ahmed, 5, AU-UNIST Photo / Stuart Price, 11

Note to Parents and Teachers

The Let's Look at Countries set supports national curriculum standards for social studies related to people, places, and culture. This book describes and illustrates Somalia. The images support early readers in understanding the text. The repetition of words and phrases helps early readers learn new words. This book also introduces early readers to subject-specific vocabulary words, which are defined in the Glossary section. Early readers may need assistance to read some words and to use the Table of Contents, Glossary, Read More, Internet Sites, Critical Thinking Questions, and Index sections of the book.

Printed and bound in China.
970

TABLE OF CONTENTS

Where Is Somalia?

Somalia is a country in Africa.

It is nearly as big as

the U.S. state of Texas.

The capital city is Mogadishu.

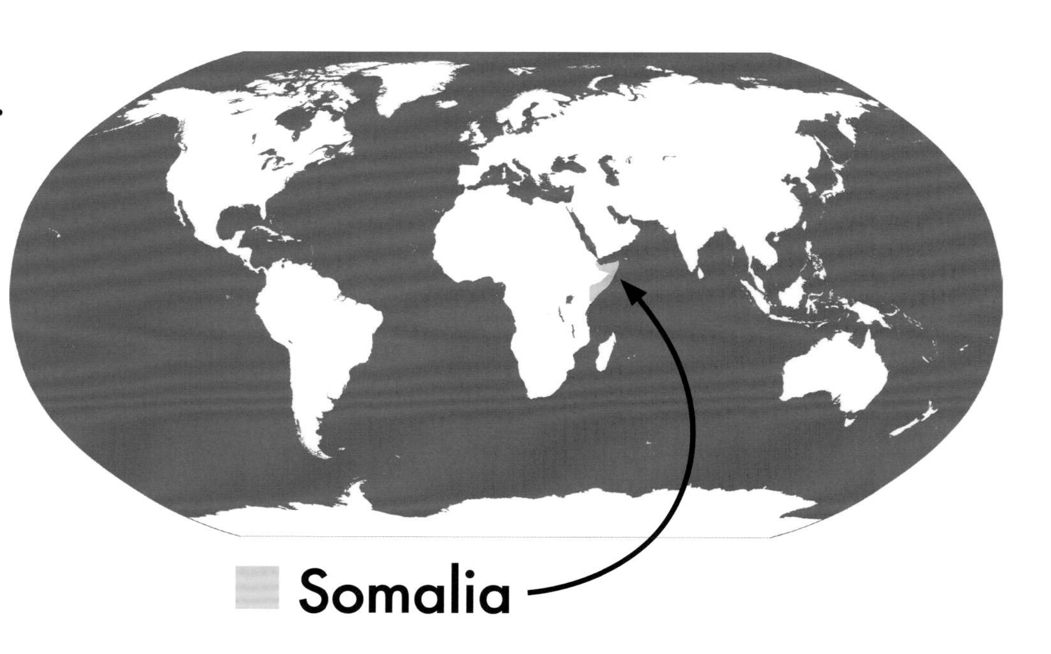

Mogadishu, Somalia

From Deserts to Mountains

Much of Somalia is flat desert. There are mountains in the north. The climate is hot. Somalia does not get much rain.

In the Wild

Some big animals live in Somalia.

Lions hunt in the grasslands.

Camels walk across deserts.

Hippopotamuses lie in the rivers.

lions

camels

People

People in Somalia speak both Somali and Arabic. Families usually have more than five children. Most people in Somalia live in small villages.

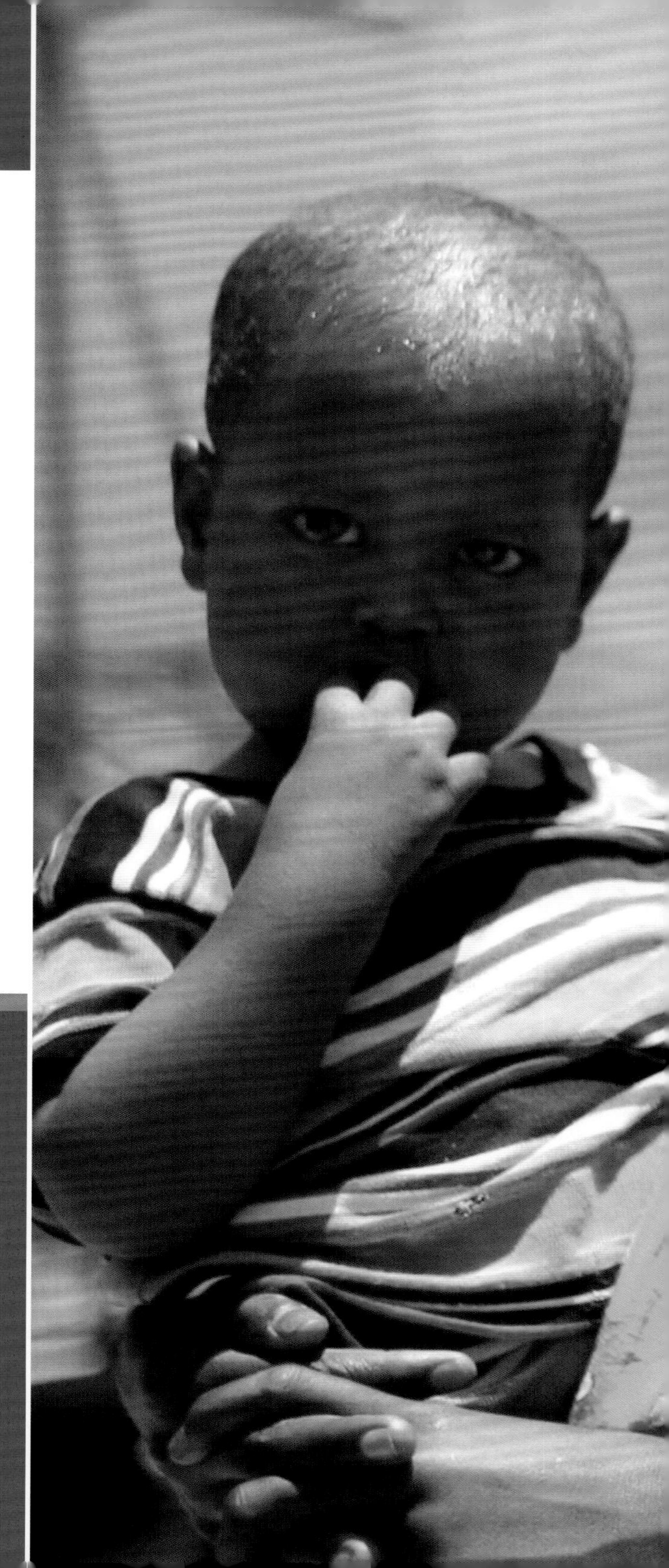

At the Table

Milk is a popular drink. Somalis drink cow, camel, and goat milk. People living by the sea eat fish. For breakfast, Somalis eat pancakes called anjero.

anjero

Festivals

Everybody is invited to weddings. They dance and sing. In July, Somalis celebrate summer. They build bonfires, splash water on each other, and dance.

On the Job

Many Somalis look after camels and cattle. Others catch fish or work on large banana or sugarcane farms. In cities, Somalis work in factories.

bananas

Transportation

In the countryside, people ride
camels and donkeys to go places.
Only a few roads are paved.
People ride buses for longer trips.
In the city, some people drive cars.

Famous Site

Laas Geel is a group of caves in northeastern Somalia. They have rock paintings of people and animals. These paintings are more than 5,000 years old.

QUICK SOMALIA FACTS

Somalian flag

Name: Federal Republic of Somalia
Capital: Mogadishu
Other major cities: Hargeysa, Berbera, Kismaayo
Population: 11,031,386 (2017 estimate)
Size: 246,201 square miles (637,657 sq km)
Language: Somali and Arabic
Money: Somali shilling

GLOSSARY

capital—the city or town in a country where the government is based

celebrate—to do something fun on a special day

climate—the usual weather that occurs in a place

bonfire—a big outside fire

hippopotamus—a large African animal with thick skin and wide jaws; hippos eat plants and swim in water

READ MORE

Markovics, Adam. *Somalia.* Countries We Come From. New York: Bearport Publishing Company, 2018.

McDonald, Joe. *African Wildlife.* Animals in the Wild. Broomall, Penn.: Mason Crest, 2019.

Owings, Lisa. *Somalia.* Exploring Countries. Minneapolis: Bellwether Media, Inc., 2015.

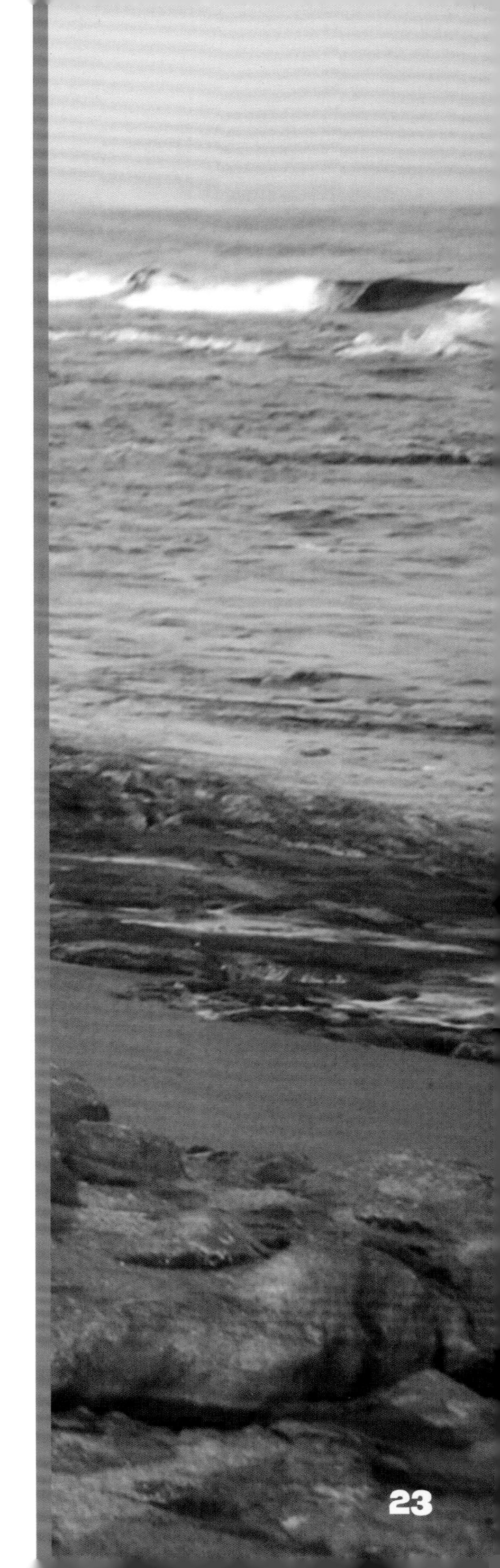

INTERNET SITES

Use FactHound to find Internet sites related to this book.

Visit *www.facthound.com*

Just type 9781977103857 and go.

CRITICAL THINKING QUESTIONS

1. Why do the Somalis who live by the sea eat a lot of fish?
2. What is the capital of Somalia?
3. Why is a desert dry?

INDEX